The Procrastination Cure

How to Stop Being Lazy, Maintain Productivity and Achieve More all the Time

Gillian R. Sullivan

All Rights Reserved. No part of this publication may be reproduced in any form or by any means, including scanning, photocopying, or otherwise without prior written permission of the copyright holder. Copyright © 2014

Table of Contents

Procrastination and What it Means
- What is procrastination and what does it mean?
- Why do people procrastinate?
- What do I do after I've figured out "the why" behind my procrastination?
- How do emotions weigh in on procrastination?

Quick Tips For Fighting Procrastination

A Ten Step Guide For Handling Tasks Without Procrastination

Long Term Tips For Beating Procrastination
- Self-Help Tip #1 – Managing Your Time
- Self-Help Tip #2 – Acknowledge And Reward Yourself For Your Accomplishments
- Self-Help Tip #3 – Organizing Your Schedule And To Do List
- Self-Help #4 – Overcoming An Overstuffed Schedule

Dealing With Procrastination In The Heat Of The Moment

Procrastination and What it Means

There are many subjects that make the cut for self-help books, all of which hope to provide you with insightful tips that are meant to help you overcome many of life's obstacles. That's because most of the problems that you have the opportunity to face are problems that many other people have faced before you. The first thing that anyone that's looking to embark on a journey for self-improvement should remember is the fact that they are not alone. Many people before you have experienced and overcome procrastination, and many people will experience and overcome it after you. It's human, and once you realize that it's not something to be ashamed of, it'll be easier for you to work on overcoming it.

What is procrastination and what does it mean?

That is a great question; but what is procrastination? To make a long story short, procrastination is the act of putting off an essential task until a later date. During the process of procrastination, often times other non-essential tasks are done in lieu of more important ones. While the actual definition of procrastination might seem fairly simple, the effects are often times not. Let's be honest; we've all encountered the pesky problem that is procrastination at one point or another. It's one of the easiest bad habits to pick up, and it usually isn't that big of a deal. Most people that procrastinate just put things off until the last minute, but they still get the job done in the end. That breeds a sense of security, knowing that even if you do end up waiting, you'll still get it done. However, if left unchecked and to its own devices, what might seem like a minor annoyance or just a bit if free time before tackling a project at first can quickly blossom into something much more serious, even to the point where overcoming your procrastination can actually be one of the biggest challenges you'll have to face; because the dangerous thing about procrastination is the fact that it is highly addictive. Just think about it; what could be better than not doing the things that you know that you're supposed to do? Do you have homework from your least favorite class to do? Forget about it! Go play some video games, because the homework isn't due for another few days anyway. Do you have dishes in your sink that need to be cleaned? Forget about them! It's not like they're going to grow legs and walk away if you leave them sitting for a while. It's easy to see how it would be more fun and less stressful to just put things off.

Take a moment to think about modern society. Everyone always has a to do list that never ends, whether it be filled with business, play, or a combination of both. People drink coffee and down caffeine shooters, trying to make sure that their bodies and minds can physically handle the amount of stress their daily work load provides. It's sad to say really, but you might not even have a moment to spare for quiet pondering, and the reasoning is simple; it's because today's society is so fast-paced. While the amount of time within a day is the same as it was twenty years ago, the amount of "time" within a day is not. Sometimes, it feels like as the years roll by, human beings as a whole feel as though they need to do more things in their lifetime. This sets the stage for it being detrimental that we know how to manage what time we do have efficiently and procrastinate as little as possible. If you already have less time in the day than you need in order to accomplish all of your goals, procrastinating will only ensure that you fail to complete the things that you set out to do. For reasons unknown, we as human beings experience an emotional reaction to the thought of having to do something that we'd rather not do or something that we've convinced ourselves that we're simply incapable of doing. One must learn to recognize this reaction because, if we aren't even aware of it to begin with, there's little we can do about it. This is one of the first steps on the journey to stopping procrastination. Before you can expect to be able to beat the demon that is procrastination, you have to understand the feelings and thoughts that lead to it. You can learn how to help yourself within the moment, but it's more productive to beat the problem at the source instead of batting it away when its symptoms flare up.

Not dealing with your procrastination can be something that's potentially life-altering , and I don't mean for the better, either. Ignoring the problem puts you at a disadvantage because you can't expect anything to change if you aren't willing to accept that you need to change it. Procrastination is one of the many different types of personal problems that won't fix themselves, especially if it has already escalated to the point that it can be considered a habit. Fortunately, there are many effective ways for overcoming procrastination and it's not something that you have to suffer through. Not breaking this bad habit, however, can have severe consequences on your life in addition the lives of those around you. Procrastination is dangerous when it gets really serious, because it can affect your physical and mental health as well, especially if it is left unchecked and unhindered.

Why do people procrastinate?

Before we can tackle the larger issue of procrastination, we must comprehend why we do it. There are a couple of fundamental reasons:

1. Feeling overpowered with a circumstance.
2. Surrendered trust that a circumstance could be changed or influenced.
3. A fear of failure.
4. Too "occupied" to accomplish the crucially important things finished.
5. Can't settle on a choice.
6. Exhausted, tired.
7. A need to stay away from work you dislike.

Each of these could be lessened down to the joy/torment rule which says that we do things to increase joy and to dodge torment. What takes after is a strategy to overcome hesitation on the things that matter and to cast off overabundance gear in your schedule that just serves to weigh you down.

But if it's such a bad habit, then why do people procrastinate? Well, as is the case with many problems, there are several reasons and factors that are involved. No two people are alike, therefore there are an infinite number of reasons for why any one person might procrastinate. One of those most common reasons is that we tend to put things off because we don't enjoy doing them. If the task at hand is something that you find unpleasant, what is there to motivate you to do it? However, despite the fact that we don't necessarily enjoy these tasks, it doesn't mean that they aren't necessary for us to accomplish. And we know it too, deep down, but we can still manage to persuade ourselves into putting things off.

Another common reason for procrastination is the belief that we simply cannot perform the task at hand, alluding to a general belief in a lack of ability. If you can't do something and you really feel as though you can't do it, then why bother? Nobody likes to feel like a failure, and the idea of facing that can be terrifying to some. It's also possible that perfectionism can set the stage for procrastination, because we might think that if we can't accomplish a task 'perfectly' that we might as well not even attempt it at all. If you're going to do something, you want to do it right the first time. So maybe you don't have everything that you need to accomplish the task at hand, or you're inexperienced in some way and feel like it would be better if you just waited until you knew that you would do an appropriate job.

While these are not the only possible reasons behind why a person might develop the habit of procrastination, they are a few of the most common. However, no matter what the reason behind it is, it's crucial that we identify why we have the tendency to put things off until the very last minute; or even to put things off completely. If you know why you're procrastinating then you can better decide what you need to do in order to fight the urge to put things off.

Take a moment to think about the things that you find yourself procrastinating about most often. Are these work-related activities? School? Home? Personal? Once you've identified some of the most common things that you are willing to set aside and put off for later, think about how those activities and tasks make you feel. If I told you to get up and do them right now, what is your first thought? Why would you rather put these tasks aside, or why do you not want to do them? Do they seem too difficult? Too time consuming? Too physically or mentally draining? Take some time to really think these questions over, and come to terms with where your procrastination problem is coming from.

What do I do after I've figured out "the why" behind my procrastination?

Once you've determined why you have a tendency to put things off, you can begin the process of doing something to change it. While the solution to your procrastination problem might not come to you in a miraculous or immediate way the moment you figure out where your procrastination stems from, you'll be in a better position to come up with one. Once you locate the source of your procrastination, you can start to fight it. Because there are so many different reasons to procrastinate, there are just as many ways to get over the habit. If you don't know why you procrastinate, then you may end up wasting time and raising your frustration through failed attempts at improvement. Imagine you're walking down the street and you trip. If you turn around and walk the same path without locating whatever it was that made you trip, it's likely that you'll trip again. But if you look down to acknowledge whatever was in your way, you can avoid it when you walk that path again.

Once you have an answer to your question, your next goal is to start thinking of ways to overcome your procrastination habit. It's no secret that every person is different so it shouldn't come as a surprise that there are a variety of different reasons for people to procrastinate, and some means for conquering the habit are more effective for a particular set of individual than others. I can give you all the helpful tips and tricks that I have in my own arsenal, but nobody knows you better than you. Therefore, you're likely to be the person that comes up with the best solutions for yourself. When you read through this self help guide, remember that you're doing this for yourself. Take my advice in kind and jot down notes on whatever you feel is most important, but don't lose sight of the fact that you are the expert here; not me. Overcoming procrastination involves overcoming those basic instincts to put off or avoid tasks. You are going to know why you do it better than anyone else, and you are going to know what advice will work best for you. Not everyone reacts the same way to everything, so don't feel like you have to force yourself to try every trick in this book. This is about you. You are the number one priority here, and you make the executive decisions. Just remember that that also means that you are the one that is responsible for making this work. You are the one that has to put forth the effort. Reading this book isn't going to help you unless you commit to change.

In the same vein as the last paragraph, some people are going to have to put forth more effort than others; depending on every individual's particular situation, overcoming the habit of procrastination can be something that can be solved with means as simple as a little bit of self-analysis or as much as therapy. That is why it is so important and crucial to figure out what the source of your procrastination is, that way you can better decide how to get a handle on it in a way that will best suit your needs. Everyone is different, so for some people, the pull towards procrastination is stronger than it is for other people. Don't feel discouraged if it feels like you have to put more time and effort into getting results than it looks like other people do. Again, this is about you. You are the top priority here.

How do emotions weigh in on procrastination?

Some people are going to have to come to terms with the fact that there are emotional undertones that they are refusing to acknowledge in the midst of the bigger picture of why they put things off. They'll have to spend time evaluating themselves and seriously questioning the feelings they experience that are caused as a result of a particular task. Some people are going to have to come to grips with the fact that they are obsessive perfectionists. If you're one of those people, you shouldn't be putting that level of stress onto yourself; because it's impossible to perform each and every single task perfectly one hundred percent of the time! Working ourselves up like that doesn't accomplish anything and can even accomplish less than what we would have originally if we weren't as stressed. We also have to recognize that there are things in life that we just aren't good at but as a result of that, our self-worth isn't lessened. The important thing is that you try to change for the better, and no matter how many times you trip or stumble, pick yourself back up and try again. If one technique isn't working for you, move on to another one. Don't feel bad if something doesn't turn out the way that you expect it to. You're not going to be able to predict one hundred percent of this process, so there will be surprises. Just stick to it.

Take a look at the task of organizing your finances, for example. While this isn't something that you're probably thrilled about having to do, it's necessary nonetheless. If you aren't good at balancing your finances, this is something that you're going to have to admit because doing so will allow you to convince yourself that spending a few extra hours on your finances is a better alternative than fretting over them and putting them off. You might also want to think about having someone that you trust look them over when you're done, just to be sure that you got everything right. That's something that you might not have thought to do, had you not admitted to yourself that you weren't very good at it.

In almost every case of procrastination, there is an emotional aspect, at least to some extent. A common emotional response in a situation like this is fear and if we learn how to take that fear out of the equation, the odds of getting a handle on the situation are considerably better. The next time you've got something that you know needs to be done and you start getting the urge to put it off to a later date, don't give in. If you find yourself wanting to find another task to occupy yourself with instead of getting the more critical one at hand done, stop. Take a step back and remind yourself why it is that you need to get the particular task done. After considering the job at hand and coming to the conclusion that it's an important one, you could potentially find comfort in the fact that you could gain something by completing it instead of putting it off.

Throughout the process of overcoming the habit of procrastination, you have got to be realistic about it, but that doesn't mean losing sight of positivity. If you don't think overcoming your procrastination habit immediately is possible, don't worry; in the majority of cases, it's not going to come that miraculously and some difficulty is something that's to be expected. As a result of the basic nature of humans, you're inevitably going to find yourself putting off a couple of things. There is no magical cure that will immediately satiate your need to put things off. Focus on the positive aspects of your quest, because it's these victories that are going to make you feel like all of this effort is worth it. Who wants to keep doing hard work if they don't feel like it's paying off? Trying to remain positive is a very critical part of the process, because it keeps you pumped and ready to keep working. Think of your positive thoughts as your own personal cheerleaders; they'll tell you that you're doing well and bring happiness at the sense of accomplishment that a job well done provides. It's much more difficult to want to put forth the effort if your head is full of negative thoughts, and it could easily leak into other aspects of your life. No matter what the speed of your journey towards conquering procrastination is, you never want to feel like you're failing. And you're not. Moving forward is moving forward, no matter what the speed, and trying to improve your procrastination habit is better than just ignoring it and pretending it doesn't exist. No matter what, you've taken the first step.

If you find yourself feeling that you're fairly good at getting some things done and still putting off a few others, don't worry about it because it's natural and isn't a cause for alarm. It's normal to continue to procrastinate one thing or another during the process of overcoming it and procrastination at this level isn't a threat to you, your well-being or the potential well-being of those around. That being said, you still have to be mindful of procrastination.

Quick Tips For Fighting Procrastination

If you happen to be an unending procrastinator, you know the torments and stress that accompanies putting things off. Despite the fact that you may have the craving or need to perform something, getting the inspiration to do it is a whole different matter. Luckily, beating your habit of repeatedly stalling is not difficult to do when you really put your brain to it.

Make a schedule. Yes, make yourself a schedule with check boxes and everything. Rundown everything, of all shapes and sizes, that you need to accomplish for your whole day and take big tasks and cut them into more diminutive bits if important things that you need to do during your day. At that point, as you work during your time mark off each of the things on your rundown. You will feel a developing feeling of pride as you outwardly screen your steadily reducing rundown of tasks. Center your rundown on including the things you commonly put off, not the things you are certain to do all the time. In the event that vital, set time spans for your things to be carried out by. For instance, rundown "take the pooch for a stroll by 12:30" instead of just "walk the puppy." Reevaluate your rundown partly during your time to rank your things focused around most noteworthy necessity. At that point, handle the most paramount ones before thinking once more at the littler things to do. Keep a journal by hand before you begin your workday. Record each belief that surfaces amid work. Each and every thing that you will eventually have to do or things you need to do at that particular minute. Don't do it, put it on a rundown and do it later. This keeps you from getting into the "procrastinating zone".

Complete the hard stuff. When you have an approaching task that's making you stall and causing you to be ineffective in different zones, tackle it first. Completing the biggest thing on your to do list of things to do will make you feel additionally profitable and provide a sense of support that will make you want to do different things you've been pushing to the side. In the event that a bigger task on your list is something that isn't possible in one sitting, make a rundown of little parts of it that you can fulfill today. Break the assignment into more diminutive sub-tasks. Doing this will make it less overwhelming and make it easier for your brain to really begin. Don't stress over finishing the whole thing, yet make strides now so that doing so later on is a breeze. Make an extreme schedule for this single extend, and have it put some place you will see it all the time. As you stamp things off you will be inspired to keep doing thus, and seeing it all the time will remind you that your venture needs to be carried out.

Perform two-minute tasks. At whatever point you are displayed with something that you would prefer not to do or would consider putting off, ask yourself "will this take me short of what two minutes to complete?" For a number of us, this incorporates little errands like taking out the rubbish or pulling a couple of weeds, yet can incorporate basic assignments in every aspect of life. Anything that you need to put off however takes two minutes to do - do it. Just compel yourself to utilize the following 120 seconds to be profitable and do the obligation you ordinarily would push off for quite a long time or days.

Make a timed work schedule. On the off chance that you end up being pulled off into the profundities of fantasies, set a portion of time to only do work. Take ten minutes and evacuate all diversions - your telephone, magazines, or considerations of your appealing affection - and go into a working furor. Energize yourself to work profitably for ten minutes, and afterward do a reversal to whatever it was you were doing. Chances are, you'll get into a score and continue working at a high pace actually when your free for all times out. Attempting to a clock is by and large viewed by most masters as being one of the most ideal approaches to create train toward oneself and stop procrastinating. The most acclaimed technique for attempting to strict time controls (known as time-boxing) includes making a to do list of the tasks at hand. Each one task is then allotted an accurate measure of time to finish. In the event that you don't complete the errand in the designated time, then you proceed onward to the following one. Utilizing this work game plan strengths you to make a move, as you can't stand to waste whenever.

Don't forget how to show yourself a bit of mercy. On the off chance that you can't center and are working half-heartedly at your tasks, don't give yourself a hard time. It's alright to make mistakes, miscalculate, or find out that you aren't capable of completing the task at hand in the time you estimated for it. Set a clock for ten minutes, and sleep, read a book, or call your companion. Do whatever it is you've been thinking about while you've been staring off into space so that the enticement is evacuated once you return to work. Just make sure to finish in time for your due date as opposed to overlooking it when your lack of caution wears off.

Uproot your diversions. Despite the fact that it may appear as though calling your mother or reading up on the following section of text in a book that's irrelevant to the task at hand are things you must fulfill within a brief span of time, they're most likely simply distracting you from accomplishing your work. Put on some noise canceling earphones, turn off your telephone, and shroud your distractions (books, your guitar, cleaning, whatever it might be). In the event that you have an issue with web surfing while you're chipping away at your machine, take a stab at utilizing a specific machine application that constrains your web utilization. Rescuetime is an application that closes off certain (or all) sites for a specific measure of time that you set, and must be voided if your machine is turned off. You can download it for nothing on the web. In the event that your issue is concentrating on composing an enormous paper or work report, take a stab at utilizing the Ommwriter program. This is a statement preparing program that totally closes out your screen (counting the taskbar at the lowest part) and plays delicate instrumental music or repetitive sound help you think. You can download the most essential variant for nothing on the web.

Don't be too dead set on being a perfectionist. In case you're sitting tight for the ideal time, the ideal supplies, or you won't stop until you've "consummated" your venture, you're putting off finishing your undertaking. Keep away from this "flawless is necessary" thinking by considering amount over quality. In the event that your venture doesn't oblige flawlessness however in any case you're centered around it, stop and proceed onward to your next assignment. When you've got done with all that, you can backtrack and wrap up your unique errand.

Inspire yourself. Numerous individuals claim that the reason they stall is because they think that they work best under pressure. So what do you do if your activities don't have any due dates? Make your own. Set yourself due dates to complete some work. It's extremely important to the success of how journey to being able to quit delaying tasks and get to be more productive.

Set a period that you must finish your undertaking by, and either compromise with yourself at the end of that time or set up a backup action for yourself in the event that you aren't effective in your attempt to fulfill your goal time. Remotely force due dates. Have you recognized that due dates that are given from an alternate source are more successful than due dates that are given and enforced by yourself? A simple case in point would be the deadline of a job given to you by your manager or educator versus an extra credit task that you're doing on your own time. Utilize your creative energy in whatever capacity you need to in order to make sure that you can force due dates on yourself remotely. One good thing to do would be to ask your companion to call you at the end of the due date. You can also go for a more independent way of thinking like testing yourself to complete the task and if it's not done on time, then you will toss 20 bucks, or an alternate sum as per the necessity of the errand, into some kind of funding for the city or give that cash to you want to donate to an individual or philanthropy that you would like to support, on the off chance that it would be hard for you to approach your companion to do it for you.

Encouraging feedback is the best method for persuading yourself to want to get things done. Provide yourself with a treat to anticipate as a prize for locking in on your schedule; go see a film, consume a chocolate bar, go out with a companion, whatever it is that will propel you. Have a go at utilizing negative support - taking ceaselessly something terrible - as a helper. For instance, promise yourself that on the off chance that you complete your exposition by Friday night, you won't need to run your errands, do your tasks, or whatever it is that you would prefer not to do. In the event that support isn't working for you, utilize discipline as a help. Use negative discipline - taking endlessly something great - to invest and work more energy. Don't let yourself take that rest, consume your supper, or complete your most loved book until your errands have been carried out. For the most extreme samples of delaying, put your cash hanging in the balance. Give somebody you trust a certain measure of your free cash, $50 for instance, and let them know to use it on themselves on the off chance that you don't complete your undertaking by a certain time; or just tell them to hang onto it until you finish. Along these lines, you need to work so as to keep your well-deserved cash in your pocket.

Get an assistant. On the off chance that you can't deal with your own, discover a companion or relative to help you work. Have them sway you to stay on task and help you when you require it. Informing somebody about what you have to do will persuade you to complete your task, on the grounds that on the off chance that you don't you will need to endure the humiliation of letting it out to them. Set up a couple of hours of time where you go around and finish all your tasks with a companion. Thusly, you will have somebody with you while you work to keep you centered and on track. Schedule check-ins with your trusted friend so that they can call to see where you're at. These might be due dates for specific tasks, at which point you will either be applauded or chastised by your companion focused around your advancement report.

Concentrate on the final objective. It's not difficult to see just the titan to do list of things to do, as opposed to the nervousness free feeling of achievement at having completed them. As you work, concentrate on all the available time, unwinding, cash, whatever it might be that you get when you complete. This will help you to stay on errand and work towards your objective.

Do one task at a time. Despite the fact that it appears as though multitasking is accomplishing more work in a little measure of time, however multi-taskers are regularly wasteful and do substantially less work. So work on doing one thing at once and don't overpower yourself with errands. Assume that it is more productive to complete the current workload rather that hopping to an alternate assignment without finishing the first, because for most people, it is.

Break your to do list down into pieces. Even if you don't physically write down each task as littler portions, think about it while you do it. Yes it's true that there are numerous task that are big enough to push us off of the track, this is a direct result of the procedure called 'Transient marking down' which says we are more prone to try for a prize which is more fast approaching than for one which is far later on. Simply put; you're more likely to want to want to put forth the effort to reach for the goal that is closer than one that it much further away. It also helps organize what you're doing in your head, making the task easier because it helps you reach your ultimate goal by breaking it down into smaller steps. Little remunerates like TV , Facebook and so forth give us a little unavoidable prize.

Attempt the Pomodoro system; work for twenty-five minutes and treat yourself with a break of five minutes or/and some little remunerate like a scaled down nibble. Rehash the cycle again until the undertaking is finished. The Zeigarnik effect says when we begin a new assignment, our mind has envisioned how the undertaking will be carried out and the brain will continue interfering with us until we complete the errand.

Remember to think about the positive things that will come from completing the task at hand. You can even write down the pros of doing the current task on a bit of paper to make sure that you can look over at it when things get particularly difficult to continue. If you can keep the benefits of completion in mind while you're working, you're more likely to want to complete it. It's like hanging a carrot in front of a cartoon rabbit while it runs on a treadmill; it'll keep you going.

A Ten Step Guide For Handling Tasks Without Procrastination

You have a due date approaching. And again you find yourself sitting around and as opposed to doing your work, you are fiddling with various things like checking email, online networking, viewing features, surfing web journals and gatherings. You know you ought to be working, yet you simply don't feel like doing anything, and so you decide not to force yourself.

Most of us are all very well acquainted with the dawdling sensation. When we linger, we waste away our available time and put off vital assignments we ought to be doing them till its past the point of no return. Furthermore, when we realize that it has come to the point where it is without a doubt past the point of no return, we panic and wish we had begun earlier. The constant procrastinators I know have invested years of their life circled in this cycle; postponing, putting off things, slacking, escaping work, confronting work just when its unavoidable, then rehashing this circle once more. It's an unfortunate propensity that consumes us and keeps us from accomplishing more prominent brings about existence.

Don't let hesitation assume control over your life. Here, I will impart my individual steps which I use to overcome stalling with incredible achievement. These ten steps will doubtlessly apply to you as well:

1. Break your work into little steps. A piece of the motivation behind why we hesitate is on the grounds that subliminally, we discover the work excessively overpowering for us. Separate it into little parts, then concentrate on one section at the time. In the event that you tarry on the task in the wake of separating it, then separate it much further. Before long, your ask will be simple to the point that you will be considering "gee, this is simple to the point that I should do what needs to be done now because it won't take long at all!" For sample, I'm right now I'm writing this book, which is a grand undertaking as a whole. Book composing at its full scale is a huge task and might be overpowering to some. It certainly is for me. On the other hand, when I separate it into stages --for example; (1) Research (2) Deciding the theme (3) Creating the blueprint (4) Drafting the substance (5) Writing Chapters (6) Revision (7) and so forth, all of a sudden it appears to be extremely

reasonable. What I do then is to concentrate on the quick stage and accomplish it to my best capability, without deduction about alternate stages. When it's set, I proceed onward to the following.

2. Change the atmosphere. Diverse situations have distinctive effect on our profit. Take a gander at your work area and your room. Do they make you need to work or do they make you need to cuddle and slumber? In the event that it's the latter, you ought to investigate the idea of changing your workspace. One thing to note is that an environment that makes us feel motivated before may lose its impact after an amount of time. On the off chance that that is the situation, then now is the right time to change things around.

3. Make an itemized course of events with particular due dates. Having only one due date for your work is similar to a reason to dawdle. That is because it gives us the ability to afford the feeling that we have time and hold pushing everything once again, until it's past the point of no return. Break down your undertaking (see tip #1), then make a general course of events with particular due dates for every little errand. Thusly, you know you

need to complete each one assignment by a certain date. Your courses of events must be strong, excessively – i.e. in the event that you don't complete this by today, it's going to imperil everything else you have arranged after that. Thusly it makes the direness to act. My objectives are broken down into month to month, week by week, directly down to the every day undertaking records, and the rundown is a call to activity that I must achieve this by the indicated date, else my objectives will be put off.

4. Wipe out your lingering pit-stops. On the off chance that you are tarrying on the verge of being exposed to too much, that might be on account of you making it easy to get distracted. Recognize the distractions that take up a considerable measure of your time and move them into a different space that is less available. Impair the programmed notice alert in your email customer. Dispose of the preoccupations around you. I know some individuals will take off the beaten path and erase/deactivate their Facebook accounts. I think it's somewhat radical as tending to stall is more about being aware of our activities than balancing through tying

toward oneself systems, however in the event that you feel that is what's required, put it all on the line.

5. Hang out with individuals who move you to make a move. I'm almost certain on the off chance that you use only ten minutes conversing with Steve Jobs or Bill Gates, you'll be more motivated to act than if you used the ten minutes doing nothing. The individuals we are with impact our practices. Obviously investing time with Steve Jobs/Bill Gates consistently is most likely not a plausible system, yet the guideline applies. Recognize the individuals/companions/partners who trigger you – doubtlessly the go-getters and diligent employees – and hang out with them all the more regularly. Before long you will instill their drive and soul as well. As a freelance writer, I hang out with rousing word masters by perusing their sites and relating with them consistently by means of email/social networking. Its correspondence through new media and it lives up to expectations all the same.

6. Get a pal. Having a partner makes the entire process significantly more fun. In a perfect world, your mate ought to be somebody who has his/her own particular set of objectives. Both of you will consider one another

responsible to your objectives and arrangements. While it's redundant for both of you to have the same objectives, it'll be far and away superior if that is the situation, so you can gain from one another. I have a decent companion whom I converse with consistently, and we generally get some information about our objectives and advancement in attaining those objectives. Evidently, it goads us to continue making a move.

7. Enlighten others concerning your objectives. This serves the same capacity as #6, on a bigger scale. Tell all your companions, associates, acquaintances and family about your undertakings. At some point during any time that you see them, they are sure to get some information about your status on those activities.

8. Search out somebody who has effectively accomplished the result. What is it you need to achieve here, and who are the individuals who have achieved this as of now? Go search them out and unite with them. Seeing living evidence that your objectives are extremely well achievable in the event that you make a move is one of the best triggers for activity.

9. Re-elucidate your objectives. On the off chance that you have been delaying for a developed time of time, it may reflect a misalignment between what you need and what you are right now doing. Regularly, we exceed our objectives as we find all the more about ourselves, yet we don't change our objectives to reflect that. Make tracks in an opposite direction from your work (a short get-away will be great, else simply a weekend break will do as well) and take sooner or later to regroup yourself. What precisely would you like to accomplish? What would it be advisable for you to do to get there? What are the steps to take? Does your current work adjust to that? On the off chance that it does not ,what would you be able to do about it? Stop over-muddling things. Is it accurate to say that you are sitting tight for a flawless time to do this? That possibly now is not the best time due to X, Y, Z reasons? Dump that thought in light of the fact that there's never a flawless time. In the event that you continue holding up for one, you are never going to perform anything.

10. Compulsiveness is one of the most compelling motivations for tarrying. At the end, it comes down to

making a move. You can do all the strategizing, arranging and conjecturing, yet in the event that you don't make a move, nothing's going to happen. Infrequently, I get onlookers and customers who continue grumbling about their circumstances, and then they decline the opportunity to make a move at the end of the day. The world has a rude awakening for people like that: I have never heard anybody stall their approach to accomplishment before and I am certain that it's never going to change within a brief span of time. Whatever it is you are lingering on, in the event that you need to accomplish it, you have to get it together and do it.

Long Term Tips For Beating Procrastination

You may or may not be wondering what you can do as far as long-term prevention goes now that you've read about the basics of procrastination. If the former is true in your case, keep reading. Short-term prevention tips are great for in-the-moment situations, but you don't want your efforts at combating your procrastination to go in vain and as a result, long-term prevention tips are something that you should seriously consider looking into.

Self-Help Tip #1 – Managing Your Time

In order to keep yourself on track, you've got to have good judgment as far as the management of your time goes. This is one of the most basic pieces of advice that anyone can give you when it comes to beating procrastination. Simply put, when you procrastinate, you waste the time that you have in front of you that you could be using for the tasks that you need to complete. It's a simple failure to efficiently take care of tasks in the amount of time that you have available. Say, for instance, that you've only got two hours of free time to finish reading this book. If you put it down and decide to go do something else, you're procrastinating, and by doing so you're wasting that time. In the end, you either will choose not to finish reading this book, or you'll end up waiting until the last minute and that will add stress that we all know isn't fun or necessary. Managing your time in an organized and clear manner will alleviate that problem, so long as you stick to your schedule.

Now, that doesn't mean that you need to plot and schedule every waking moment of your day. Everyone has their own desires and needs, so the level in which you choose to organize and schedule your time should be based on what you need to do and how badly you feel you need structure in order to get it done. Inevitably, some of us are going to procrastinate more than others. If that's your case, you're going to have to work at overcoming the habit on a daily basis by working a little at a time, because it's not something that can be conquered all at once if your procrastination is built on a large scale.

Self-Help Tip#2 – Acknowledge And Reward Yourself For Your Accomplishments

Every time you manage to resist the urge to procrastinate something, even though you'd rather put the task at hand off until a later date, it's a good idea to reward yourself a little and acknowledge the accomplishment. Even if you didn't completely finish the task, it's better than not doing it at all and you can still give yourself a pat on the back for making an effort and that is a job well done in and of itself. This goes back to the emotional connection between you and your procrastination. By positively reinforcing the fact that you tried, successfully or otherwise, you are reminding yourself that you are taking steps forward, and that it is a good thing. Steps forward are always welcome and worthy of praise. The next time you want to procrastinate, you'll be able to think back to the last time that you rewarded yourself, and it will urge you to resist the temptation to push tasks aside.

Think about it; would you rather do all of the dishes and then reward yourself with your favorite dessert, or would you rather just do the dishes and not get anything for it at all? If you're looking at a sink of dirty dishes and all you can think about is the work, you're less likely to want to do it. But if you look at a sink full of dirty dishes and see a delicious portion of savory, mouth-watering dessert in your future, the difference is obvious. By rewarding yourself for a job well done, you're reinforcing positive behavior and telling yourself that it is a good thing to get things done. But you're not just rewarding yourself in the moment, you're giving yourself incentive.

In the beginning of your journey to overcoming your procrastination habit, it's a good idea to set short-term goals. You have to make sure that the short-term goals that you set for yourself are both realistic and timely. In this case, 'realistic' translates to making sure that the goals that you've set for yourself are actually short term and not overly ambitious. As opposed to just saying "I'm going to get it done," try adding some time and telling yourself something to the effect of "I'm going to get it done by Wednesday or I'm not going to watch any television," instead because in that case, your goal automatically becomes more realistic than it was initially.

The next things to do is to make sure that you're keeping your goals as specific as possible, especially because they're short terms. For example, "I want to make good grades in school," is not a very specific goal and neither is "I want to make a good grade in math during the second semester." They're very vague. What is the definition of 'a good grade?' However, goals that are specific are thoroughly studying and completing all assignments and these small goals can build up to the larger goal of making good grades. If you allow loopholes to form, you'll inevitably find yourself beginning to make excuses that prevent you from your completing your goals, resulting in more of a procrastination than you had to begin with. In order to be successful in fighting this battle, you're going to have be firm with yourself, buckle down and get things done.

Next, you should provide yourself with something simple that will allow you to keep track of the goals you set for yourself. Some people have found that they prefer using technology like tablets or palm pilots. However, it's very possible that using technology can create dependencies in addition to the fact that it's easier to get distracted with other applications than it is to get distracted by something more simple, such as an index card or a post-it note. If the index card/post-it note goes in a wallet or purse that you already take everywhere with you, then the details of your goals are already easily at hand.

As you complete each goal, you should mark them off. While this may not seem very important initially, you'll find that it is easier to get things done when you know for sure what you have and have not completed. In addition, this habit is a good one to pick up because it determines whether or not you're actually looking at your list because more often than not if you do not, you'll find yourself only looking at your list if you're adding something to it and if you aren't actually looking at your list, it's easy for you to begin procrastinating. It's easy to forget that you have so many things to do when you stop reminding yourself.

If you find yourself not being helped by short-term goals at all, it's possible that you're suffering from a form of procrastination that should be examined more closely and treated by a doctor that will assess why you procrastinate in the first place with the tools of psychology. You also might find it helpful to have a third party look over your goals and offer constructive criticism, something that you should be open to due to the fact that it's more likely that a third party is going to pick up on flaws that are preventing you from accomplishing your goals than you are. Lastly, you have to remember that no amount of goal-setting tips are going to miraculously make you an effective goal-setter; this is something that is entirely up to you and your success depends on whether or not you're ready to put forth the effort necessary to get a better handle on your procrastination habit. It's one thing to write down what you have to do, but it's not going to get done unless you actually step up to do the things that you list.

Self-Help Tip #3 – Organizing Your Schedule And To Do List

Many individuals utilize some form of timetable as their every day schedule. The majority of us learned to log our schedules into calendars without really paying attention to the fact, however some have surmised that is an awful approach to arranging. There is a need to demonstrate industry standards to utilize your timetable all the more productively together with your schedule. Each has it capacities and obligations, yet they can work extraordinary in amicability once you know how. On the other hand, there are a few weaknesses to this methodology. For instance, imagine a scenario where you need to book a get-away however you don't know precisely when. Where would you put this then?

First, let's talk about how to use utilize a calendar. You can utilize a divider calendar or programming, it doesn't generally make a difference. The usefulness is the same, yet we find that utilizing programming datebook will give more adaptability and is more efficient. Particularly when you utilize it together with a schedule, as you will read later. Just remember that if one of your problems with procrastination is an affinity for distractions, using technology to organize your schedule might only end up adding to your problem.

So what ought to go in your calendar? There are a few basic things that should be put into your calendar, things that you can schedule and pinpoint exact times and dates for:

- Appointments (dental specialist, classes, supper with companions, gatherings, and so on).
- Deadlines (delivering report, documenting duties, and so forth).
- Events (pay day, birthdays, occasions, bundle landing, and so on).
- Time delicate errands (purchasing something before store shutting time).
- Center time (when you set time aside to chip away at something critical and nobody can exasperate you).

You should really consider your calendar timetable sacred ground. Nothing goes on your calendar unless it is an unquestionable requirement and can be considered time sensitive. That is the reason we encourage you to put arrangements there (clearly) and due dates in light of the fact that they are both things that happen at a particular day and time, where something needs to happen. Don't put things on there that have arbitrary or discretionary due dates. This will add an unnecessary amount of clutter into your calendar and that will make things more difficult for you to figure out how to handle it all. You don't want to overwhelm yourself, this is supposed to make thing easier. For instance, let's say that you need to book a get-away to Maui, yet you don't have any idea yet about when you need to do it so you simply put it on Tuesday at 7pm. Attempt to stay away from calendar things like this. Instead, put those things in your more flexible to do list and then work to figure out when you can accomplish the task.

Once again, I will repeat that your calendar is sacred. Just put in the vital things that you need to proceed with in a time sensitive manner. Then we can learn about the most proficient method to utilize a schedule or assignment chief.

Even though the amount of things that the average person tries to do within their day to day lives has grown dramatically through the ages, there are very few people who know how to properly use a to do list or calendar these days. It's much easier to end up procrastinating when you don't have a clear way to look at the things that you need to accomplish. It's also easier to forget certain things, which will make you feel safer in putting things off.

These days people have such a wide variety of things on their plates that they want to do that it is extremely unlikely that they can do every one of them on every single day; particularly things that can't be done inside the following week(s) or month(s), yet of course they still have to be done sooner or later. Where do you keep this data? Believe it or not, the answer is on your to do list.

Your to do list and your calendar should be two separate things. When looking at the two names that I used for them, it's easy to get confused. Your calendar is where you put all of your non-flexible and time sensitive tasks. Your to do list is where you put all of the things that you have to do, but don't have a specific time limit for. This will help you organize the tasks at hand and prioritize when need be. It'll also help you feel less overwhelmed by stopping you from cluttering up one organizational device.

You have to audit your schedule at least once a week to make sure that it stays current and up to date. That weekly point is when you should take the time to look over your schedule and see which tasks need more consideration, which might be completed and can therefore be erased, and which assignments could be added to ventures. Keeping up your to do list is extremely essential because you will be utilizing the information that you put on it for arranging your days and weeks ahead.

Now that I have impressed the importance of a calendar and to do list, it is now the right time to demonstrate to you how compelling they could be together as assets. The beginning stage of arranging is realizing what duties you have to worry about right now. Once you've figured out what tasks you have to organize, you can see which of those belong on your to do list and which can be put on your calendar to be dealt with on which days. When you're arranging and you perceive that on a Tuesday you have a considerable measure of gatherings and tasks that cannot be move, then you know that worrying about trying to complete the timeless to do list tasks on Tuesday is a terrible thought. While in the event that you perceive that on a Wednesday you don't have a considerable amount of things on your calendar, you could plan that you take a shot at particular tasks from your to do list that day. Under this umbrella of logic, you can tell when you want to try to decide which days to worry about the tasks on your to do list, you should add them to days that your calendar isn't already full of important and time limited tasks.

Remember that you need to consistently edit and correct your calendar and to do list in order to keep it accurate. It won't help you if it doesn't have the right information on it.

Utilizing a calendar and to do list together in tandem is an incredible thought, however, it does take a tad bit of practice. Trying to organize and schedule things might seem monotonous, but it really will help you learn how to better make use of your time. That is the reason we suggest you utilize scheduling as a long-term solution to your procrastination problem.

Self-Help #4 – Overcoming An Overstuffed Schedule

If you're looking at a calendar and to do list that's stuffed so full that it makes your head spin, it might be more difficult for you to want to beat procrastination. When there's so much to do, it feels like you've got a list of things to do that never ends, and it feels like you're staring down at shackled wrists. If you literally have no free time for fun in your schedule, it makes sticking to your schedule more difficult. There's no way around that feeling other than cutting down the tasks that you've set out for yourself.

Get clear about what you need in life. Procrastinators, you'll cherish this! Take twenty to thirty minutes to do this brisk objective arranging activity. Record all your objectives in some of life's biggest categories like: vocation, training, connections, money related, physical, outlook, inventive, profound, open administration, travel, relaxation, and other. When you have written up a rundown of what you want with your life, then whittle it down to your main ten, then down to your main five, and afterward your main three. Do this by asking yourself, "Would I be able to live without this?" Let your less vital objectives lie torpid on a "possibly" list that you can reconnoiter again in a couple of months.

Take a look at your to do list (not your calendar) and erase the things that don't identify with your main three to five objectives. Simply say goodbye. What's more don't think back! You can save them for another time by writing them on another piece of paper and filing them away for later, when you have more time to spare. This might sound like a form of procrastination, but it's really a useful tool for helping you defeat it.

If you can't figure out what to save for later and what to focus on right now, then get help from someone you trust. You don't have to do this alone, and sometimes a fresh perspective is exactly what you need. Choices are intense for me. I like to utilize the genius/con system and appoint focuses. I additionally prescribe getting assistance from a friend that you know is great with making decisions. When you've settled on your choices, then separate them into your current to do list and the to do list that you're holding onto for later.

Take a look at the items on your to do list that you aren't exactly thrilled to have to do and connect them to the items on your objective arranging activity. It serves to rationally (and in composing) attach these assignments to one of your fundamental objectives or qualities. So for instance, "Keeping a clean and tidy home and work area permits me to have clarity of brain which is something I cherish greatly. By having clarity of psyche I will be better ready to take a shot at my objectives and have less uneasiness." By joining the undertaking to the delight of having the capacity to think unmistakably, I now have a reason that will persuade me to make a move. This works just like the reward factor that I mentioned in a previous tip; only this time instead of creating a new reward for finishing a task, you're just opening your eyes to see that the reward was there from the start. If you can connect the tasks to positive outcomes instead of negative processes, then you're more likely to want to begin and complete them.

Plan your day every day. This is not a huge assignment and so it ought to just take around ten to fifteen minutes of calm time. Do the most troublesome and most paramount things first and work your path down to the simpler stuff toward the evening. What better way to make sure that you get as much done than to plan it all out and allot yourself time for each thing? You'll feel okay on the off chance that you do this. Plan your week simply enough to approximately plan in a percentage of the huge things you know you need to accomplish. Not planning things thoroughly can cause hesitation and stop you from wanting to begin a task.

Concentrate on the idea that your schedule is important and try to inspire yourself to want to wait to check email and such until after you've completed your first huge undertaking. If you tell yourself that you have to wait to do more personal, free time things until after you've accomplished something productive, then you're more likely to want to finish that productive something.

Try to get rest when you're tired or have low inspiration towards productivity. Don't be too hard on yourself about the timing of an assignment either, and after you've learned to feel less tense of exactly when your tasks need to be completed, you won't attempt to escape through hesitation so hard later on. Simply reschedule and try again tomorrow, or the next available moment, if you don't get to a task on your to do list.

The reason these tasks are on your to do list instead of on your calendar is because they are meant to be flexible when it comes to scheduling. There is no anti-procrastination law that says that you have to get to absolutely every task that you put on your schedule. It's not procrastinating if you just don't have time; it's okay to save yourself the stress. Just don't put it off forever or start using this as a crutch or an excuse. Take care of business, but don't overdo it. We frequently put weight on ourselves to do certain assignments more regularly than we truly need to. For example, dusting, cleaning, washing clothes, and so forth. So show yourself a bit of mercy and set a schedule for these things that is not overpowering. It'll make it more difficult to want to get to them, as well as the rest of the items on your to do list. Do think on a "need to do" premise and let go of the thought that you have to stay constantly aware of some flawless calendar. Have you ever heard of the business idea, "in the nick of time" stock? Well this is "without a moment to spare" errand administration.

Have confidence in yourself and in your capacity to achieve anything you need. On the off chance that you've lost trust, realize that you can turn things around. Discharge the trepidation of disappointment. Disappointment is simply a learning background. Steady minded individuals will win in the end. A smidgen done consistently signifies a ton over a year. In the event that you need to, simply fake your conviction until it gets to be genuine. Recollect that, you can do it!

Break down your bigger tasks into littler parts. We tarry on assignments that are dubious and undefined in light of the fact that we don't have clear guidelines on what to do next or even how to start it. Take a couple of minutes to think over how you might be able to break down a bigger errand and schedule it into your to do list in pieces. This is useful for when you are feeling overpowered. It helps you spread out a bigger, daunting task and allows you to take care of it through the completion of smaller tasks that are spread out through a couple of days.

To recap:

- Know your most essential objectives and qualities.
- Only do errands that help those objectives and qualities.
- Mentally connection assignments to the pleasurable results you look for.
- Plan your day & week.
- Do, yet don't exaggerate. Rest when required.

- Break down enormous assignments.
- Get help deciding.
- Believe in yourself!
- Don't be afraid to ask for help!

Dealing With Procrastination In The Heat Of The Moment

Procrastination is a vice that most people hate dealing with, though it happens so very often. No one wants to deal with procrastination, and the irony is the fact that most people know they are procrastinating on something, yet decide to push it off as well; which is thus procrastinating the stop of their own desire to stop the issue of procrastination. Do not fret, because there's always a solution to your procrastination issue, though it may not be as easy as you think. However, if you really want to buckle down on your procrastination, here are some simple and effective tips for the short term project that needs to be done.

There are many things that you can do to help yourself conquer procrastination as a long term problem, but that doesn't mean that the short term is any less important. A good first tip for dealing with your task at hand and taking the issue of procrastination and beating it down into the ground is to finally face the task that you need to do. It may seem like an obvious choice, but it's genuinely something that many people do not do. Sit down, turn off any and all distractions or seclude yourself away from any distractions and force yourself to do the job you need to do. Don't check your phone. Don't check your email. Don't look at social networking. Don't turn on the television. Just sit down, look at what you need to accomplish, and focus. After around ten minutes, or more, you'll start to realize that you're having an easier time focusing on what you need to get done and keeping away from procrastination is a lot easier.

Sometimes, a distraction is something that's quite helpful, though not something that will be actively bothering you, like the internet, a cell phone, or any other miscellaneous electronics. Sometimes, if you're working on a task at hand, update a friend, coworker or family, who knows about your issue with procrastination, with how you're doing so far on your project. This will make sure that you're staying on task and your designated recipient of your status updates will be enough to remind you that you shouldn't be slacking off. You might even be lucky enough to pass across a person who might shoot you constant reminders every half an hour to an hour to continue working, just in case you have strayed from your path a bit.

Having a good time-management schedule is also extremely key. It's important to reward yourself for doing a good job at keeping to your schedule that you have planned for yourself. Perhaps after one hour of your task, you can reward yourself with a five minute break and then return to your task at hand. Make sure to stick with your five minute limit on yourself, however, because it's essential not to get distracted. Time-management, goals, and proper planning is something that can easily break down the barrier of procrastination.

There are different things that keep people focused while they're working. Most people resort to playing certain types of music that calm them, or they keep a soothing tea that can keep them interested and calm while they're working for a stress-free related work position. Once you've found something that seriously zones you in while you're working on your project or task, make sure to write it down, or remember what keeps you focused so that next time you're in need to beat procrastination, you'll have ideas of how to help yourself already!

Deadlines may not be everyone's favorite things, however, setting deadlines for yourself may be a helpful idea and it makes you continue to have goals. If you settle for doing, perhaps, one third of your project in three hours, it's extremely motivating to set goals and timelines because most people can run really well on deadlines as long as they have things planned out. Please note, however, if you do not make your goal, do not be mad at yourself or discouraged. Perhaps just evaluate what you did to not make your goal. Did you procrastinate your goal? Were you distracted? Was your goal set too high? At times, we might over think what we can do, and while keeping our hopes high is great, it can also be a very bad thing because when you don't make your goals, it can cause more stress.

Goal rewards are extremely important as well, like mentioned before, if you give yourself a reward for keeping to your schedule, you will most likely be more motivated to continue on and finish the work that you need to do. Procrastination definitely cannot give you rewards and only causes more issues.

Sometimes you can find different things that can assist you in getting in the mood for your task, especially friends, coworkers or family. If you're having issues with trying to figure out where to go with a certain job, it's always good to bounce off ideas with people who understand your way of thinking. If you need to write something, look at similar pieces of works and brainstorm with a friend on how you can achieve greatness like what you had read. It's always a smart idea to pull inspiration from other people as long as you make sure not to become a victim of copyright infringement or plagiarism. Once again, it's good to take inspiration from other work to make sure you can stay focused and beat your procrastination habits, however, stealing ideas that are not your own is not okay in the slightest bit. Generating new ideas gets you excited to work on them and can bypass the procrastination that you keep suffering from.